A QUINTET BOOK

Published by Chartwell Books
A Division of Book Sales, Inc.
PO Box 7100
Edison, New Jersey 08818-7100

This edition produced for sale
in the U.S.A., its territories
and dependencies only.

ISBN 0-7858-0481-1

This book was designed and produced by
Quintet Publishing Limited
6 Blundell Street
London N7 9BH

Creative Director: Richard Dewing
Designer: James Lawrence
Photographer: Andrew Sydenham

Typeset in Great Britain by
Central Southern Typesetters, Eastbourne
Manufactured in Singapore by Eray Scan Pte Ltd
Printed in China by Leefung-Asco Printers Ltd

CONTENTS

INTRODUCTION

Christmas is a joyous time for sharing and celebration, for fun and festivity for all the family. Decorating the house ready for Christmas is an age-old tradition that is enjoyed with much enthusiasm today. Holly, ivy, and natural forms have for centuries been used as embellishments for the festive season. However, the Christmas tree itself was popularized in Britain during the 19th century by Prince Albert, Queen Victoria's husband. Indeed, the Victorians took great delight in crafts of all kinds and used the Christmas celebration as an ideal opportunity to display their skills. During recent years Christmas has become a rather commercialized occasion. Stores are crammed with a vast array of ready-made decorations, cards, and gifts, and sadly many people have never experienced the joy and satisfaction of making their own special decorations and tokens. This year, create a Christmas to remember, using this book as your guide and inspiration.

The 13 projects contained in this book will teach you a variety of simple craft skills and imaginative ways of using them, from simple paper folding, paint effects, and dough craft to stenciling, sewing, and wreathmaking; projects using metal and wire are also included. Each project has a comprehensive equipment list, step-by-step instructions, patterns, templates, and handy tips or alternative ideas. A wide variety of materials is featured, ranging from paper, card, and fabric to metal, wire, and natural forms. The crafts require different skill levels: some are simple enough for children to help with or to do by themselves while others are a little more complicated, but all of the projects are designed with the beginner in mind.

Learning a new craft is fun, an activity for you and all the family to enjoy, and also a wonderful opportunity to experiment and to use your imagination.

Happy Christmas!

BASIC EQUIPMENT AND MATERIALS

HARDWARE

SCISSORS. Have a selection of scissors ready for all your craft needs. Use small embroidery scissors for fine work, larger, general-purpose scissors for paper and card, large dressmakers' scissors for cutting out fabrics, and finally pinking shears for making decorative zigzag cuts and neatening raw fabric edges.

TIN SNIP AND WIRE-CUTTER. These are tools used for cutting tougher materials, such as metal, wire, or even twigs or plant materials that would damage the blades of your ordinary scissors.

CRAFT KNIVES. Scalpels and craft knives are used, with a metal ruler, for cutting straight lines and for cutting out tricky areas where scissors would not be suitable. A channeling knife can be used to cut grooves. A scalpel with a swivel blade is invaluable when cutting stencils. Have a blunt kitchen knife handy for scoring and cutting floral foam.

CENTER PUNCH. A small metal gadget used for punching holes in metal or thick card.

COOKIE-CUTTER, CANAPÉ-CUTTER. Useful for cutting small shapes from dough or as a template.

HAMMER. Used with center punch and for inserting eyelets.

LEATHER PUNCH. A useful tool for punching holes in paper, card and fabric. The star-shaped part revolves, enabling you to cut six different-sized holes.

RULER. A plastic ruler for general use and a metal one for using with a scalpel or craft knife.

SAFETY FIRST

- Be careful when using sharp blades, scalpels, knives and scissors.
- Always use a thick card pad to protect your work surface when using scalpels or hammers.
- Use glues and spray paint in a well-ventilated room.
- Never leave candles unattended when lit. Always place them on a heatproof surface.
- Some of the projects in this book are simple enough for children to help with or to do by themselves, but children should be supervised when they are using scissors or craft knives.

PAPER

We are very lucky today to have a magnificent selection of paper and card to choose from for craft purposes. A variety of mat and metallic-finish papers and cards are readily available in craft stores, together with textured and corrugated materials, and more unusual handmade papers. It's great fun to experiment with different color and texture combinations. Remember to keep scraps for small projects such as greetings cards and gift tags.

OTHER MATERIALS

FABRIC. Build up a store of fabric pieces and scraps to use for sewing projects. Fabrics that do not fray easily are particularly useful.

RIBBONS. Ribbons are available in many different colors, patterns and widths. Use them as decorative trims or as functional ties and bows.

STRING AND RAFFIA. A more natural form of decorative trimming.

SEWING THREAD. Always have a supply of colored thread at the ready. Sewing projects look much more professional when matching threads are used.

PINS AND NEEDLES. Use long, fine pins to hold your work in place. Have a selection of needles for use with regular sewing thread and thicker ones suitable for embroidery floss, string, or raffia.

WIRE. Useful for wreathmaking, and floral or dried arrangements.

BUTTONS, BEADS AND METAL TRIMMINGS. Use these small trimmings to add that special finishing touch to your projects.

TIP
• Don't throw anything away. It may be useful! Save scraps of fabric, ribbon, paper, card, odd buttons, and beads, and use them to make your craft projects unique and interesting.

ADHESIVE TAPE AND GLUE

There are many different ways of joining craft materials together. The success of your project often depends on choosing the correct one.

ADHESIVE TAPE. Double-sided tape is featured in many projects in this book. It is useful for joining paper, card, and fabric. Masking tape is low-tack and is usually used for temporary joining or for masking off areas. Clear tape can be used for paper or card but do not use it where the tape will be seen.

DOUBLE-SIDED ADHESIVE PADS. These are small foam pads with a strong adhesive on both sides, suitable for joining most materials.

GLUE. Water-based glues are suitable for card and paper but you will need to use a stronger glue for fabric, beads, or sequins. There are numerous specialty glues available for individual craft purposes, including those for metals and plastics.

VELCRO. This is a very clever form of fastening. The Velcro strip has lots of tiny loops on one side and hooks on the other; when pressed together, they hold quite firmly. Velcro is available in sew-in and self-adhesive form, and a combination of both for use with paper, card, and fabric.

PAINTING AND COLORING EQUIPMENT

CRAFT PAINT. Acrylic paints are ideal for craft purposes, as they are quick drying and easily diluted. They can be cleaned up with water when wet but are permanent when dry.

SPRAY PAINT. Useful for painting delicate or intricate articles.

PENS AND PENCILS. Use soft pencils for sketching design lines or making tracings. Thick marker pens can be used for decorative purposes.

BRUSHES. Have a variety of brushes to apply both paint and glue. Always make sure to clean brushes thoroughly after use.

TOOTHPICKS AND SKEWERS. Useful for supporting craft items while they dry and for piercing holes, stirring paint, and applying glue.

MIXING PALETTE. For mixing small quantities of paint or glue, though you can use an old saucer or dish for this.

SPIRAL PAPER GARLAND

Simple and colorful paper garlands to festoon the Christmas tree or decorate a room.
The garlands are very effective when made from two different colored papers, and can
easily be joined together to form longer strands. The folding method may be a little tricky at
first but when mastered it is quick and easy to do. Children can help with this too.

1 Lay the sheets of paper on top of one another on a piece of thick card. (The card is used to protect your work surface from damage from the cutting blade.) Mark the cutting lines on the paper very lightly with a pencil about ¾ inch apart. Then, using the scalpel or craft knife and the metal ruler, carefully cut the paper into strips.

2 Take two different colored paper strips and place the ends together. Snip across the ends at an angle of 45 degrees.

You will need
◊ Large sheets of thin colored paper
◊ Metal ruler
◊ Craft knife or scalpel
◊ Pencil
◊ Double-sided adhesive tape
◊ Thick sheet of card

SAFETY FIRST

• Always take extra care when using a sharp cutting blade or scalpel. Use a metal ruler as a guide to cutting straight lines and also to make sure that the blade doesn't slip.

3 Separate the two strips. Then turn the top strip over and attach to the first, using a small triangle of double-sided adhesive tape. The strips will form an inverted V-shape.

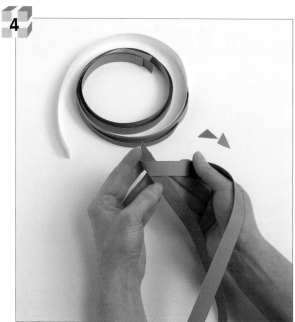

4 Carefully fold the first strip from left to right over the top strip. Press the fold firmly between your forefinger and thumb. Fold the second strip over the first in the same way, rotating the whole thing slightly clockwise as you go. Continue folding in this way.

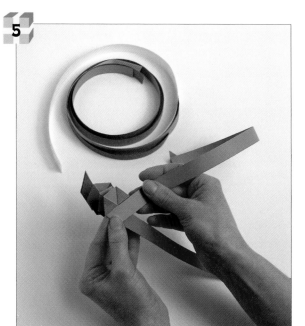

5 As you fold, the strips will form a little hexagonal shape. As you continue, the spiral garland will be formed. When you reach the end of the paper strip, simply join on another, using a small piece of double-sided adhesive tape.

DECORATED GIFT WRAP

This year, wrap up the Christmas gifts in your own hand-decorated paper.
Plain mat poster paper can be transformed into a richly patterned and unusual gift wrap
using very simple painting techniques.

DAPPLED EFFECT PAPER

1 Lay the sheet of poster paper on a flat surface. Pour a small amount of gold paint onto a small saucer or mixing palette. Take a piece of tissue paper (you could use a piece of cloth) approximately 8 inches square and crumple it up in your hand. Press the crumpled surface of the paper onto the paint in the saucer. Do not overload the paper with paint.

2 Press the paint-coated surface onto the poster paper to create the mottled pattern. Do this all over the paper, using a light dabbing action. Take care not to smudge the paint as you go.

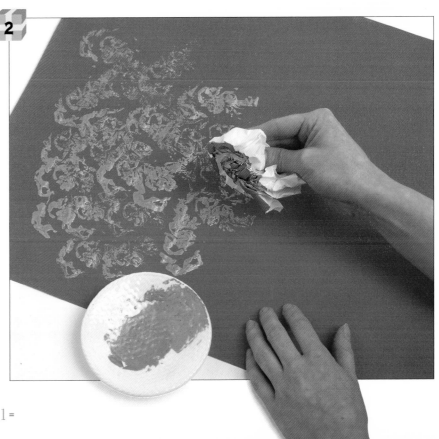

You will need
◊ Large sheets of plain mat poster paper
◊ Onion skin paper or tissue paper
◊ Scissors
◊ Ruler
◊ Masking tape
◊ Gold poster or acrylic craft paint
◊ Metallic gold spray paint
◊ Corrugated card to match poster paper

TIP
• Why not experiment with different colored paints and background colors? Or use a combination of techniques to create your own individual patterns?

STRIPED EFFECT PAPER

1 Lay your poster paper on a flat surface and place masking tape in diagonal stripes about 1 inch apart.

2 Apply gold paint, using the dappling technique described on page 11. Wait for the paint to dry a little before carefully removing the masking tape.

CHECK EFFECT

1 Take a sheet of poster paper and fold it up like a concertina or a fan. Make the folds about ¾ inch wide. Stretch out the folded paper sheet a little and place it on your work surface. Using the metallic gold spray paint, coat the paper with a fine mist of color. If you spray from one angle, only one side of the fold will catch the paint, creating a striped effect when the paper is opened out.

2 When the paint is dry, repeat the process but this time folding the paper at right angles to the first folds. This creates a check effect.

Add that special finishing touch with matching gift tags, pretty folded fans, and strips of corrugated card.

> ### SAFETY FIRST
>
> • Always read directions carefully when using spray paints. Use them only in a well-ventilated room. Protect or mask off other surfaces while spraying.

CHRISTMAS CRACKERS

These shiny Christmas crackers will insure that your celebrations go with a bang!
Made from metallic-finish crepe paper, they add a touch of luxury to the Christmas dinner table.
Make one for each guest with a special gift inside.

You will need
◊ Metallic-finish crepe paper
◊ Scissors
◊ Pinking shears
◊ Pencil
◊ Double-sided adhesive tape
◊ Toilet tissue inner tubes
◊ Cracker snaps
◊ Matching narrow ribbons

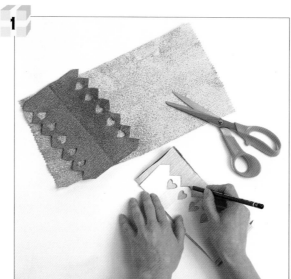

1 Trace the templates on page 41. Cut one rectangle measuring 13⅛ x 7 inches from one color crepe paper, and two pieces measuring 7 x 6¼ inches from a contrasting color paper. Always cut the crepe paper so that the grain will run along the length of the cracker. Using the pinking shears, trim both short ends of the larger piece. Fold the smaller pieces in half, matching the 7-inch sides. Place a template to the fold of the paper as indicated and, using the pencil, trace carefully around it.

2 Use sharp scissors to cut out the shapes from the contrast pieces.

3 Position the contrast cut-out pieces approximately 1 inch in from the pinked edge of the larger rectangle. Attach in place with double-sided adhesive tape.

4 Take three cardboard inner tubes and trim one to approximately 4½ inches long for the center and the other two to 2½ inches long for the ends. Turn the crepe paper piece over. Place the larger tube in the center and the two smaller tubes about ½ inch in from the pinked edge. Slip the cracker snap inside the cardboard tubes. Also at this point insert a small gift or some wrapped candies into the center tube. Wrap the crepe paper around the tubes.

5 Attach the edge of the crepe paper firmly with a strip of double-sided adhesive tape.

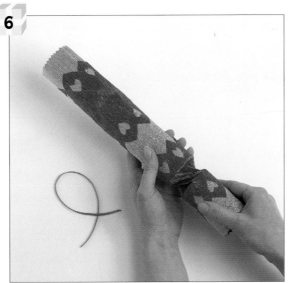

6 Hold the central part of the cracker with your left hand and one end with your right. Gently twist the cracker clockwise, then anticlockwise. This creases the paper between the cardboard tubes and makes it easier to tie in the next step.

7 Take a short length of matching ribbon and tie the cracker tightly around the creased part. Trim off the ends of the ribbon. Tie the other end in the same way.

MINI CHRISTMAS TREES

A mini Christmas tree is ideal in many homes today where space is at a premium. Use the larger
tree to brighten up a small corner, the tiny ones to make your dinner table extra special.
A humble flowerpot, some wire netting, and a few twigs are transformed with a spray of
gold paint and the addition of simple salt dough decorations and colorful ribbon trimmings.

You will need

◊ Wire netting
◊ Small wire-cutter
◊ Terracotta flowerpots
◊ Dry blackberry stalks or twigs
◊ Metallic gold spray paint
◊ Floral foam
◊ Knife
◊ Floral wire
◊ Sphagnum moss
◊ Bundle of natural raffia
◊ Tartan ribbons
◊ All-purpose flour
◊ Salt
◊ Rolling pin
◊ Small star- and heart-shaped canapé cutters
◊ Double-sided adhesive tape

1 Using the wire-cutter, carefully cut out a
trapezium shape from the wire netting. The
following measurements are approximate: larger
tree, depth 14 inches, bottom 22 inches, top
10 inches, and for the smaller tree, depth 8 inches,
bottom 12 inches, top 6 inches.

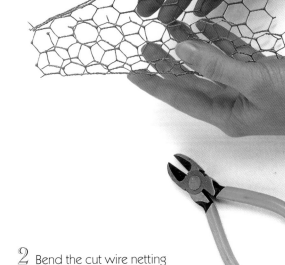

2 Bend the cut wire netting
trapezium to form a cone shape.
Twist the wires together to join the
center seam. Then snip off any untidy
ends with the wire-cutter.

SAFETY FIRST

- Always use spray paints in a well-ventilated
  room. Protect work surfaces with
  newspaper or a spare sheet of paper.
  Follow directions on the can carefully.
- Take care not to scratch or cut your hands
  on the cut wire, as it can be quite sharp.

3 Take two dry blackberry stalks or a few thin
twigs and tie them together with raffia. Spray the
stalk, pot, and wire shape with metallic gold spray
paint and let them dry.

4

4 Cut a round of floral foam to fit inside the pot snugly.

5

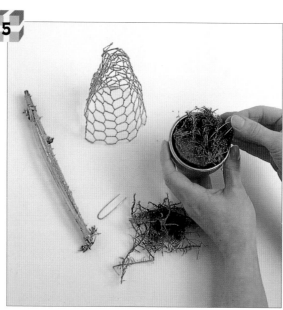

5 Place a small amount of sphagnum moss on top of the foam. Secure it into place with small pieces of wire bent into U-shapes.

6

6 Take three or four long strands of raffia and tie them together in a knot at the bottom of the wire tree shape. Wind the raffia in a spiral around the tree, tying securely at the top. Snip off any loose ends with scissors.

7

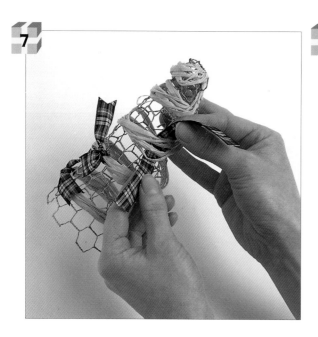

7 Using small pieces of tartan ribbon, tie the raffia to the wires at intervals all over the tree. Trim the ends of the ribbons into neat points.

8

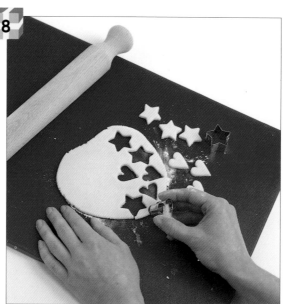

8 To make salt dough decorations, place eight tablespoons of all-purpose flour and four of salt in a small bowl and mix into a dough with about eight tablespoons of water. Knead the dough until it is soft and pliable. Roll it out on a floured board to a thickness of about ¼ inch. Cut out little heart and star shapes, using the canapé cutters. Place the cut-out shapes on a baking sheet and bake at 290°F for about 1½ to 2 hours. If the shapes are not completely dry, leave them in a warm place overnight.

The larger tree has hanging shapes around the bottom edge. Just pierce a small hole at the top of each shape with a bodkin or toothpick before they go into the oven. When the tree is finished, you can tie the shapes on with a small piece of raffia.

TIPS

- Use the dough recipe for making full-size tree decorations, using larger cookie cutters or trying your own shapes. Simply make a paper template and cut around the shape with a sharp knife.
- Salt dough can also be used to create flat and three-dimensional shapes for all sorts of other craft projects. Why not experiment a little?
- You can decorate your mini trees in a multitude of ways, with sequins and beads, pine cones or dry seed pods, dry leaves or flowers, dried fruit slices and nuts, paper cut-outs, or even shiny foil-wrapped candies.

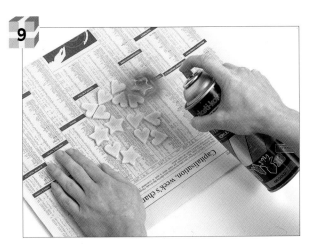

9 Spray the dough shapes on both sides with metallic gold paint and let them dry.

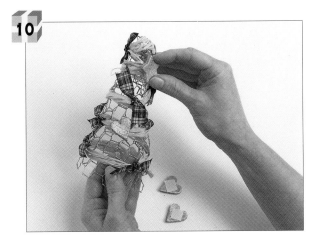

10 Attach the painted dough shapes to the tree, using small squares of double-sided adhesive tape.

11 Push the painted stalk firmly into the foam inside the pot, then place the tree over the stalk. You may need to squeeze the top edge together a little so that it stays in place.

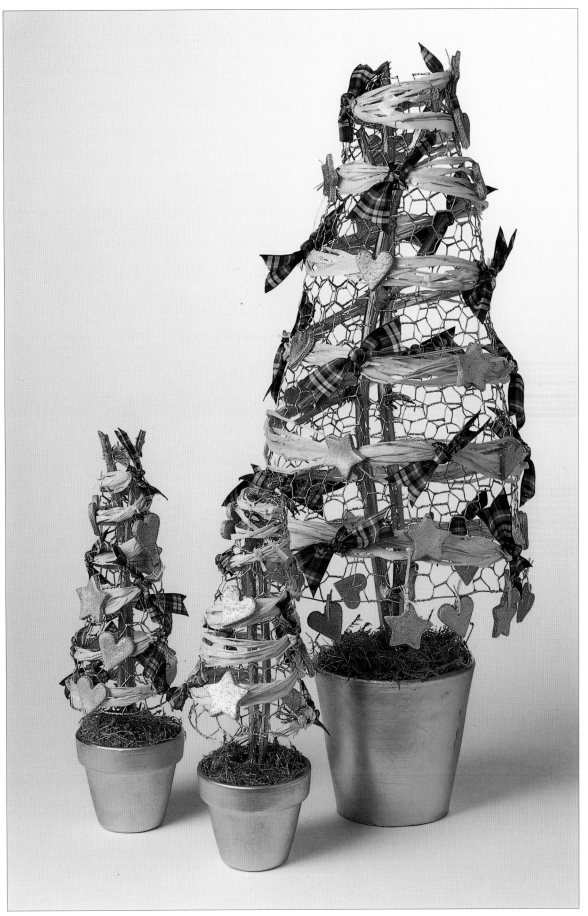

CHRISTMAS WREATH

Nature has provided the basic materials for this delightful wreath. Holly, ivy, and pine cones
are always in plentiful supply at this time of year. Hang the wreath on your front door or
use it as a table centerpiece with candles to celebrate the festive season.

You will need
◊ Long strands of variegated ivy
◊ Sprigs of holly
◊ Pine cones
◊ Small wire-cutters
◊ Floral wire

1 Taking two long strands of ivy, wind them
loosely around each other to form a ring about
12 inches in diameter.

2 Wind another three or four strands of ivy around
the bottom, tucking in the ends neatly as you go.

3 Trim the holly sprigs to about 7 inches long. Push
the stems into the ivy bottom around the outside.
Secure the holly in place with short lengths of wire if
this seems to be necessary. Take care not to scratch
your hands: the holly prickles can be very sharp!

4 Finally, wind a short length of wire around the bottom of each pine cone, leaving two prongs protruding downward. If the cones are open, this should be quite easy to do.

5 Attach each pine cone to the inside of the ivy bottom by pushing the wire prongs into the ivy bottom and twisting them together at the back, making them secure.

TIPS

• As this wreath is made from evergreen plants, it should last quite well for a week or more if kept in a cool place.

• When the foliage is past its best, dismantle the wreath and keep the pine cones for future projects.

TABLE DECORATION

Make a table decoration that is both attractive and edible. A channeling knife is used to engrave patterns into the skin of small clementines. The designs used here are very simple, but why not experiment with your own designs or use larger fruits with more surface area to decorate?

You will need

◊ 7 small, firm-skinned clementines
◊ Channeling knife
◊ Block of floral foam for dry arrangements
◊ Whole cloves
◊ Floral wire
◊ Small wire-cutter
◊ Small sprigs of fresh green foliage
◊ Large slow-burning candle

1 Hold a clementine firmly in one hand and the channeling knife in the other. Beginning at the center of the fruit, press the knife gently into the skin, making vertical lines down the sides. As you drag the knife along, it will cut a shallow groove in the skin to reveal the white pith underneath. You may need to practice a little before you begin the finished piece. Make about eight grooves in each fruit. Engrave three clementines in this way.

2 For the spiral patterns, hold the fruit in one hand and the knife in the other as before. Press the knife into the skin at the center, then gently rotate the fruit anticlockwise, cutting a continuous groove around the fruit. Engrave four clementines in this way.

3 Cut the foam into a round approximately 4 inches in diameter and 2 inches deep.

TIPS

• After engraving the fruits, keep the narrow strips of skin, dry them, and use them to add color and citrus fragrance to potpourri.

• Engrave larger citrus fruits, such as oranges, in the same way. Use them as a table centerpiece, piled up in a large bowl. Your guests can eat the oranges after dinner!

4 Carefully press whole cloves into the centers of the fruits. This gives a lovely fragrance in addition to decorative effect.

5 Using the wire-cutter, cut a 6-inch piece of wire for each fruit. Push the wire through the bottom of each fruit and bend to form a U-shape. Then push the ends of the wire into the foam bottom.

6 Trim some fresh green foliage, such as holly or another evergreen, into small sprigs. Push the stems firmly into the foam.

7 Press the bottom of the candle into the center of the foam bottom.

SAFETY FIRST

• Never leave a burning candle unattended. Always place decorations containing candles on a heatproof surface.

GIFT BAGS

These charming country-look gift bags, make perfect containers for Christmas presents.

You will need

◊ Thin white card
◊ Thin colored card
◊ Paper or card with a surface texture
◊ Check cotton fabric
◊ Pencil
◊ Ruler
◊ Knife
◊ Scissors
◊ Water-based glue suitable for fabric and paper
◊ Paintbrush
◊ Double-sided adhesive tape
◊ Leather punch
◊ Ball of string
◊ Small buttons with two holes

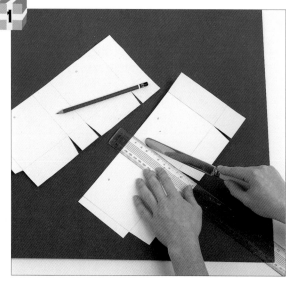

1 Trace the template given on page 42 transferring all the fold lines accurately. The template shows the two sizes. For the bag made of card, cut out a box shape in colored or textured card; for the fabric-covered bag, use thin white card. Score along all the dotted lines.

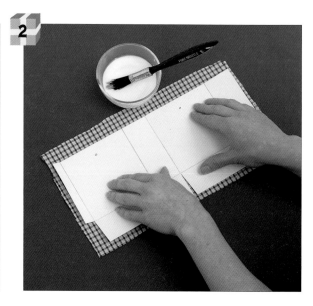

2 For the fabric-covered bag, cut a piece of fabric about 1 inch larger all round than the card shape. Glue the shape to the fabric, and smooth out any air bubbles. Trim the fabric close to the card shape, leaving the 1-inch excess at the upper edge. Crease at the fold positions again.

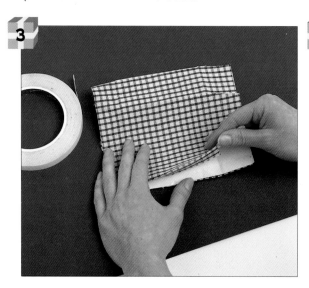

3 Attach the tab to the side edge using double-sided adhesive tape.

4 Fold in the flaps at the lower edge to form the bottom of the bag. Secure in place using double-sided adhesive tape.

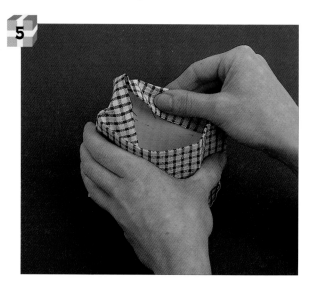

5 Apply a strip of double-sided tape to the inside of the bag around the upper edge. For the fabric-covered bag, fold down the fabric neatly.

6 For the fastening use the leather punch to pierce a hole at the center of the bag, about ¾ inch down from the folded edge.

7 To make button fastenings, first cut a 10-inch piece of string for each. Fold the string in half, then thread the ends through the holes in the button and tie in a knot. Next, thread the loop end through the punched holes at the top of the bag, then bring the loop around the button at the front. This makes a very pretty and secure fastening for your gift bag.

8 To make a fish gift tag, trace the tag template given on page 42. Cut one shape from thin colored card. Score and fold it along the dotted line. Pierce a small hole at the head end, using the paper punch. Glue on a small button for the eye. Knot on a short length of string and tie up the gift bag with a neat little bow.

TIP

- The template for these gift bags shows two sizes, but if you require a smaller or larger gift bag, simply enlarge or reduce the original on a photocopying machine.

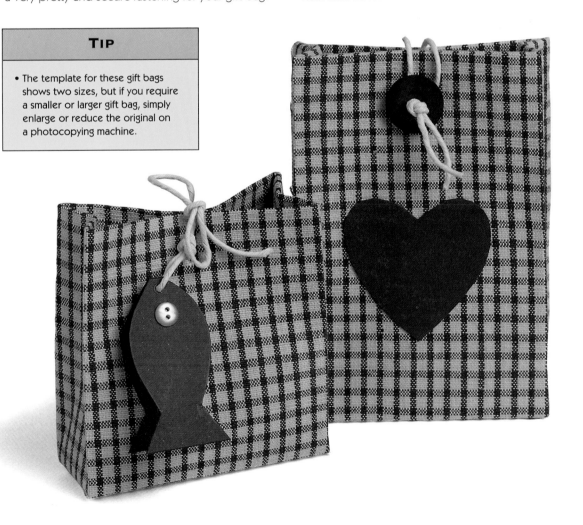

9 To make fish and heart decorations, trace the fish and heart motifs given on page 42. Cut them out in fabric or card and fix them to the front of the bag with glue or double-sided tape.

TREE DECORATIONS

Forget expensive, store-bought tree decorations this year! Make your own from some string and a few polystyrene shapes. Ours are linked together with golden beads and tassels, and have tiny star sequins that will catch the light and twinkle beautifully on your Christmas tree.

You will need
- ◊ Polystyrene craft balls
- ◊ Ball of string
- ◊ Water-based glue
- ◊ Quick-drying craft glue
- ◊ Paintbrush
- ◊ Scissors
- ◊ Quick-drying acrylic paint
  (base color and metallic gold)
- ◊ Toothpicks
- ◊ Plasticine
- ◊ Small sponge
- ◊ Gold beads and sequins
- ◊ Sewing thread
- ◊ Bodkin
- ◊ Gold thread
- ◊ Gold tassels

TIP

- If you can't find polystyrene balls, you could revamp old tree decorations by gluing string to the outside, or perhaps use an old table tennis ball for the small sizes. For a different shape, you could try using a blown egg.

1

1 Place the polystyrene ball on the end of a toothpick. This is a useful way of holding the ball steady whilst gluing and painting. Coat the polystyrene ball with a water-based craft glue. (Other glues melt the polystyrene.) Take the end of the string and wind it around the toothpick at the bottom of the ball. Slowly rotate the ball, winding the string around as you go. The string will stick to the tacky surface of the glue. Snip off the string when you reach the top. Use the plasticine to keep the string-covered shapes upright as they dry.

2

2 For the flat, round shapes, take a piece of string about 12 inches long and coat it with glue. Coil it up from the center and let it dry.

3

3 Apply one or two coats of acrylic paint to each shape. Acrylic paint is ideal for craft purposes as it dries quickly.

4

5

6

4 Pour a little of the metallic gold paint onto a small saucer or mixing palette. Take a small piece of sponge and dip it into the paint. Use a light dabbing motion to transfer the gold paint to the string-covered shapes.

5 When the paint has dried, use a quick-drying craft glue to apply tiny gold star sequins at random over the shapes. First squeeze a tiny spot of glue onto the shape, then pick up the sequin on the end of your finger, and place it gently onto the glue spot.

6 In assembling the decorations, use your imagination to create unusual effects with different combinations of round and flat shapes together with beads and tassels. First thread some beads or a tassel onto matching sewing thread. Attach the thread to a thicker gold thread loop. Make this loop long enough to go through the ball and leave enough to hang it by at the top. Thread the loop onto a long bodkin. The polystyrene is soft enough for the bodkin to pass through quite easily. If you have any difficulty, pierce the ball with a skewer or a thin knitting needle first.

PARTY HATS

Dazzling hats to put everyone in the party mood. Two colors of reflective mirror card are combined effectively, using simple shapes and a clever woven detail.

You will need
◊ Sheets of metallic mirrorcard in two colors
◊ Pencil
◊ Metal ruler
◊ Scalpel or sharp craft knife
◊ Scissors
◊ Leather punch
◊ Double-sided adhesive tape
◊ Shirring elastic

1 Trace the hat and star templates given on page 43. Transfer the tracings to the wrong side of the metallic card, making sure to mark all the cutting lines accurately. Cut them out carefully, using the scissors. Cut the hat shape and the star from different colors.

2 Cut the V-shaped lines of the woven detail, using a sharp craft knife and a metal ruler.

3 Take a hat shape and a star and begin to weave by first slotting point 3 under C, then point 2 under B, then point 3 under A. Slide the shapes together as far as they will go.

4 Lift up point 2 and tuck point C underneath it. Then lift up point 1 and tuck point B underneath.

SAFETY FIRST

• Always place work on a thick card or safe cutting surface when using a scalpel or craft knife.

5 Finally, bring point C over point 1 to complete the woven detail.

6 Using the leather punch, pierce a small hole either side of the hat shape. The position is indicated on the template. Apply a strip of double-sided adhesive tape to the tab area.

7 Tear the backing paper from the tape and secure the hat into a cone shape. Thread a 14-inch piece of shirring elastic through the pierced holes at each side of the hat and tie securely in a knot.

TIPS

- Why not use the hats as party invitations? Send the hats to each of your guests, flat in a large envelope, with the party invitation written on the back.
- The woven detail on the hat is a simple but effective way of joining two pieces of card or paper together.
- You could apply the star motif to a square or rectangular piece and use it as a greetings card. Also, using the V-shaped cuts and the same method, you could create your own shapes.

STENCILED INVITATIONS AND PLACE CARDS

Gold on ivory is a stylish color combination for these matching invitations and place cards.
This project offers four different designs for you to choose from, each requiring a different skill level.

You will need
◊ Clear acetate stencil film
◊ Pencil
◊ Scalpel or swivel-blade craft knife
◊ Leather punch
◊ Textured paper, such as a heavyweight watercolor paper
◊ Gold stencil paint
◊ Sponge
◊ Ruler
◊ Scoring knife
◊ Sharp craft knife
◊ Metallic writing pen

SAFETY FIRST

• Always take care when using scalpels or sharp craft knives. Always use a thick card sheet to cut out on or a safe cutting surface.

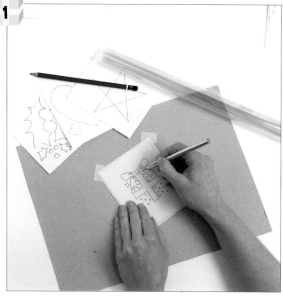

STENCILS

1 Trace the stencil templates given on page 44. Place the traced design on a thick card sheet or a safe cutting surface and place a rectangle of acetate the same size on top. Use tabs of masking tape to keep the acetate in place. Carefully cut out the design, using your scalpel or swivel-blade craft knife. The star and heart are the easiest ones to start with. The holly involves more curved lines. The gift is a little more difficult. For the gift, cut out only the ribbon at this first stage.

2 Use the leather punch to cut the tiny dots on the gift stencil. These would be too difficult to cut with a blade.

TIPS

• Always use paints that are specially designed for stenciling as they are quick-drying. This means that you are less likely to experience smudging. However, you will have to wash your brushes, sponges, and mixing palettes quite quickly, before the paint becomes too hard.
• You could stencil some matching paper napkins, placemats, and even a tablecloth for a totally coordinated look.
• Now you have mastered the art of stenciling in one color, try two colors. The gift stencil would be ideal to start with. First cut out a stencil of the ribbon only. Then cut one with the dots only. Stencil the ribbon in one color and the dots in another, but be careful to match the design. Try out your own designs when you become more confident.
• The invitations make pretty Christmas cards too.

INVITATION

1

2

3

1 Cut a rectangle of paper measuring 8 x 4¾ inches for each invitation. Mark the halfway point lightly with a pencil line. Place the stencil in the center of the left-hand portion. Pour a little of the gold stencil paint onto a small saucer or mixing palette. Take a small piece of sponge and press the surface onto the paint. Do not overload the sponge with paint: only a small amount is needed. Now press the sponge lightly onto the stencil using a dabbing action. Stenciling is very easy when you get the hang of it, but practice on a sheet of spare paper if you are unsure. Let the paint dry a little and then remove the stencil carefully.

2 Beginning at the top of the stenciled pattern, halfway across the front portion of the paper, use the scalpel to cut carefully around the right-hand side of the design. Stop when you reach the bottom, again about halfway across the front portion.

3 Using a ruler and a blunt knife, score along the halfway point. Then score halfway across the front portion, above and below the stenciled design, not across the design itself.

PLACE CARDS

Cut a square of paper measuring 4¾ x 4¾ inches for each place card. Mark the halfway point, then stencil the design as before but positioning the stencil slightly to the left of center. Score across the halfway point, again avoiding the stenciled design itself. Write a name on the card with a metallic gold pen and then fold as shown.

4

4 Fold along the score lines as shown, so the stenciled design stands out of the folded front part. This gives a very simple 3-D effect.

CHRISTMAS CARDS

Send your special Christmas greetings this year inside these unusual cards made from pieces of an old tin can! They're fun to make, and a card made by hand is always a joy to receive.

You will need
◊ Sheets of thin colored card, some with
  surface texture
◊ Pencil
◊ Ruler
◊ Scoring knife
◊ Scalpel or sharp craft knife
◊ Pieces of tin
◊ Small hammer
◊ Center punch
◊ Double-sided adhesive tape
◊ Masking tape
◊ Tin snip
◊ Protective gloves
◊ Hessian fabric
◊ Double-sided adhesive pads

The metal pieces we used came from the side of a large empty coffee can. Use the tin snip to remove the top and bottom of the can, then cut down the side and open up the can to form a flat sheet.

SAFETY FIRST

• Always use protective gloves when cutting metal, as the edges can be very sharp.
• When punching out the designs, use a thick card sheet to protect your work surface.

FRAMED MOTIF CARD

1 Trace the card templates and motif outlines given on pages 45-46 (templates given for square, rectangular and triangular cards). Make sure to transfer all cutting lines and fold lines accurately. The dots on the motif outlines indicate the punch hole positions. Cut the basic card shape, then cut out the window, using a scalpel and a metal ruler. Score and fold where indicated.

2 Choose a motif for your card, then cut a piece of tin about 1 inch larger than the motif all round. Place the metal piece on a thick card sheet, then place the traced motif on top. Hold the tracing in place with tabs of masking tape. Next, begin to punch along the dotted lines of the traced motif. Place the point of the center punch on each dot and tap once or twice with the hammer. The aim is to make a clear dent in the surface of the metal, not to pierce a hole right through. Continue until the motif is complete, then remove the tracing.

3 Using the tin snip, trim the metal piece so it is ½ inch larger than the window in the central portion of the card. Attach the metal face down behind the window, using double-sided adhesive tape.

4 Fold the left-hand portion of the card over the center to cover the back of the metal piece. Secure it in place with double-sided adhesive tape.

CUT-OUT MOTIF-CARD

1 Cut out the basic card shape but do not cut out the window. Score and fold where indicated and make up the card as before. Cut a piece of hessian about 2 x 2 inches and fray the edges. Choose a motif and punch out the design as before, then trim around the edge of the design, using the tin snip.

2 Fix the hessian square to the front of the card with double-sided adhesive tape. Fix the metal cut-out motif to the center with double-sided adhesive pads.

TIP

• If you cannot obtain suitable metal pieces, the same method can be used to punch design into metallic-finish card.

CHRISTMAS STOCKINGS

Jolly Christmas stockings ready to hang up on Christmas Eve. This project involves basic sewing
skills only, but the use of the eyelets and glossy satin ribbons lends that professional touch.
The stockings are washable and you'll be able to use them year after year.

You will need

◊ 20 inches taffeta fabric
◊ 20 inches lightweight polyester batting
◊ 20 inches red taffeta lining
◊ Scissors
◊ Pins
◊ 51 inches narrow black satin binding
◊ Sewing needles
◊ Sewing thread
◊ Gilt eyelet kit (10 eyelets for each stocking)
◊ Hammer
◊ Flat piece of wood
◊ 39 inches red satin ribbon
◊ Sewing machine (optional)

The fabric and binding amounts are for each
stocking.

1 Trace the stocking pattern given on page 47 to
full size. (Each square represents 2 inches.) Place
pattern to the fold of the fabric as indicated. Cut out
one pattern each in fabric, batting and lining. Pin the
layers together, sandwiching the batting between
the fabric and lining.

2 Open the satin binding out slightly. Pin the right
side of the binding to the lining side of the stocking
around the front and upper edges, matching the
raw edge of the binding to the raw edge of the
stocking. Take care to ease the binding around the
curves. Pin regularly at intervals of about 1 inch.
Machine stitch the binding in place or, if you don't
have a sewing machine, hand sew the binding using
a small running stitch. Try to stitch on the fold of the
binding that is closest to the raw edge.

3 Wrap the binding around the raw edge and
slipstitch the fold by hand to the original stitching
line. Try to keep the stitches as small as possible.

4 Insert eyelets in the positions marked in your pattern. (There will be instructions included in the eyelet kit.) First place the stocking on a hard surface, such as a piece of wood. Use the tool provided in the kit to make a hole at the position marked. Place the back piece under the hole and gently press through, then place the top part over the first.

5 Place the tool over the eyelet, and hammer the pieces together.

6 Fold the stocking in half along the center back seam. Then stitch the curved foot seam together, taking a seam allowance of about ¾ inch. Again, if you do not have a sewing machine, this can be done by hand, using a small running stitch.

7 Turn the stocking through to the right side and thread the satin ribbon through the eyelets, finishing off with a neat bow at the top. For the hanging loop, take another 8 inches of binding, fold it in half and stitch along the length. Then fold in half to form a loop and stitch to the inside of the stocking at the center back.

ADVENT CALENDAR

Children will love this Christmas tree Advent calendar, complete with shining star, a host of chirpy robins and a pile of little gifts. Each one hides a box containing candies or a small surprise and has a number to correspond to each of the days up to Christmas.

You will need
- ◊ Stiff card (green, white, and red)
- ◊ Pencil
- ◊ Scissors
- ◊ Double-sided adhesive tape
- ◊ Double-sided adhesive pads
- ◊ Dark fiber tip pen
- ◊ Assorted scraps of paper (brown, red, black, gold, etc.)
- ◊ Scraps of corrugated card (red, green)
- ◊ Narrow ribbons (assorted colors)
- ◊ Craft knife
- ◊ Double-sided adhesive Velcro fastening
- ◊ Adhesive numbers

1 To make the tree and background, trace the template pieces full size, using the grid given on page 47. (Each square represents 2 inches.) First cut out the snow from the white card and use double-sided tape to secure it in place on the large blue background board. Then cut out the pot from red card, and the tree from green.

2 Attach the tree and the pot to the background, using double-sided adhesive pads. This will give a slightly three-dimensional effect.

3 To make the robins, trace the robin template shapes given on page 48. You will need to make 12 robins. Cut the main body in brown, the wings in black, and the chest in red. Remember that the robins need to face each other, so make six that look to the left, and six that look to the right.

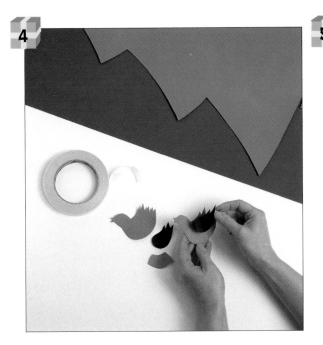

4 Assemble the robins, using double-sided adhesive tape.

5 When the robins are complete, draw in the eyes with a dark fiber tip pen.

6 To make the boxes, trace the box tray and sleeve templates given on page 48. Cut 24 trays in white card, 13 sleeves in green card and 11 sleeves in white. Score and fold where indicated. Make up the box trays and fix with double-sided tape.

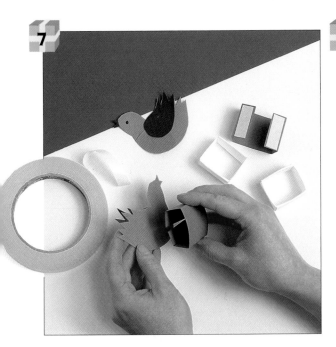

7 Using double-sided tape, attach the green sleeves as shown to the back of the robins and the star, and save the white ones to attach to the gifts (step 8).

8 To make the gifts, cut six squares 2¾ x 2¾ inches and five rectangles 2 x 2¾ inches from stiff white card. Cover the squares and rectangles with scraps of corrugated card, paper, foil, or wrapping paper, then tie each with a ribbon bow. Attach a box to the back of each gift as before.

9 Cut 24 pieces of Velcro, each ½ inch long. Separate the hook side from the loop side and fix one to the back of each box sleeve and the other to the calendar. Use the photograph as a guide to positioning.

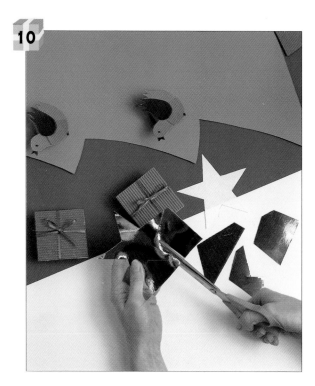

10 Trace the star template given on page 48. Cut out in gold card and attach a box to the back.

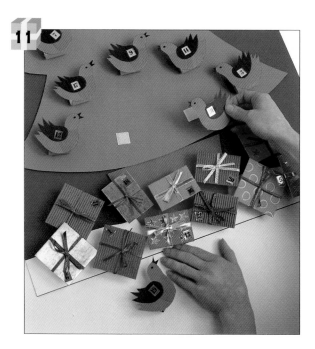

11 Stick a number on each of the robins and the gifts but make the star number 24. Secure each piece in place on the calendar, and then count the days to Christmas!

TEMPLATES

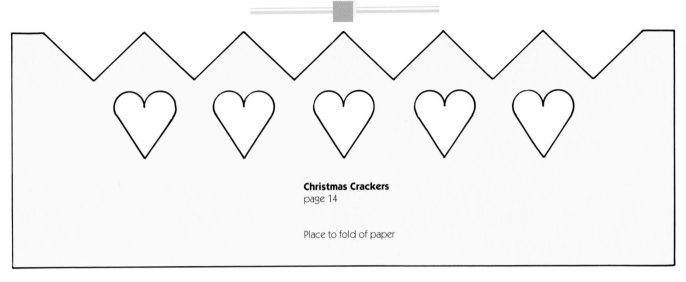

Christmas Crackers
page 14

Place to fold of paper

Christmas Crackers
page 14

Place to fold of paper

Christmas Crackers
page 14

Place to fold of paper

Large Bag

○

Small Bag

○

Gift Bags
page 24 (2 sizes)

Cut along solid lines
Score and fold along dotted lines

Tab

Gift Bag Heart Motif

Fold

Gift Bag Fish Tag

Gift Bag Fish Motif

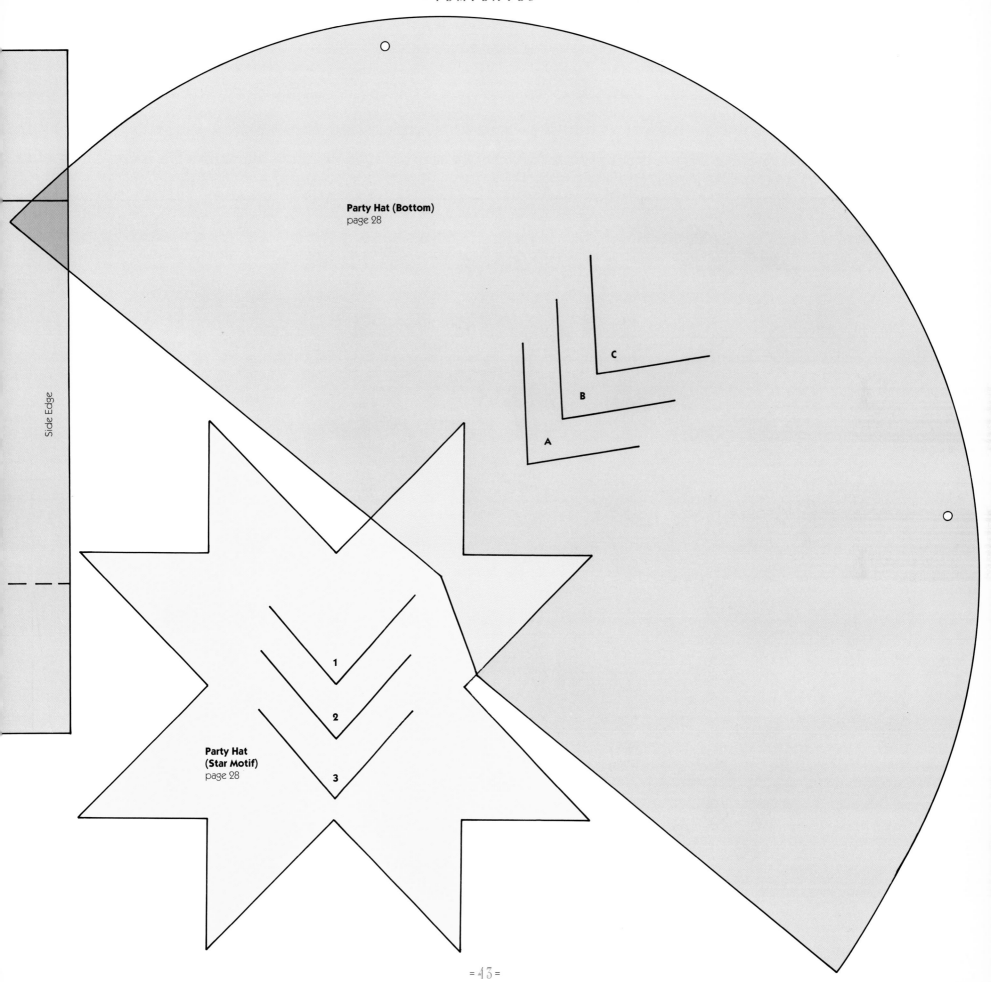

Party Hat (Bottom)
page 28

Side Edge

C

B

A

Party Hat
(Star Motif)
page 28

1

2

3

Stenciled Invitations and Place Cards
page 30

Heart

Star

Holly

Gift

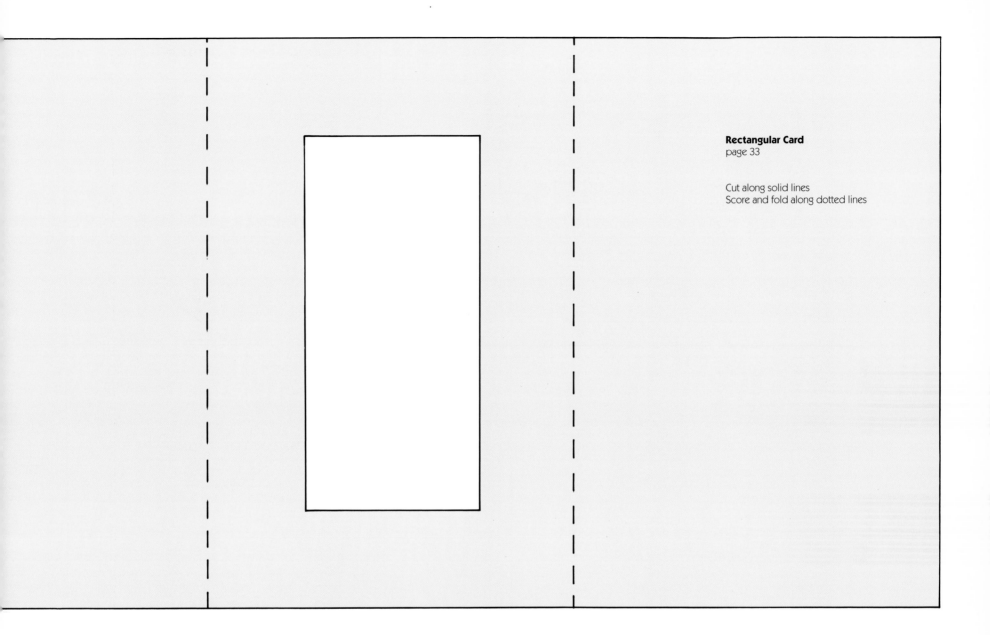

Rectangular Card
page 33

Cut along solid lines
Score and fold along dotted lines

**Christmas Cards
(Punched Tin Motifs)**
page 33

Dots show punch holes

Triangular Card
page 33

Cut along solid lines
Score and fold along dotted lines

Square Card
page 33

Cut along solid lines
Score and fold along dotted lines

**Christmas Cards
(Punched Tin Motifs)**
page 33

Dots show punch holes

Christmas Tree Advent Calendar (Tree)
page 38
Each square represents 2 inches

Christmas Stocking
page 36
Each square represents 2 inches
Pattern includes ¾-inch seam allowance around foot seam
Dots indicate eyelet position
Cut a piece each for fabric, lining and wadding

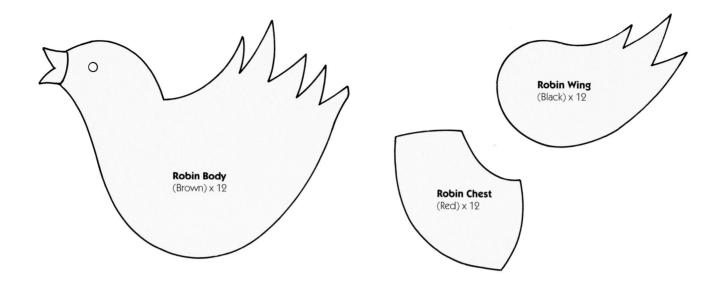

Robin Body
(Brown) x 12

Robin Wing
(Black) x 12

Robin Chest
(Red) x 12

**Christmas Tree Advent
Calendar (Motifs)**
page 38

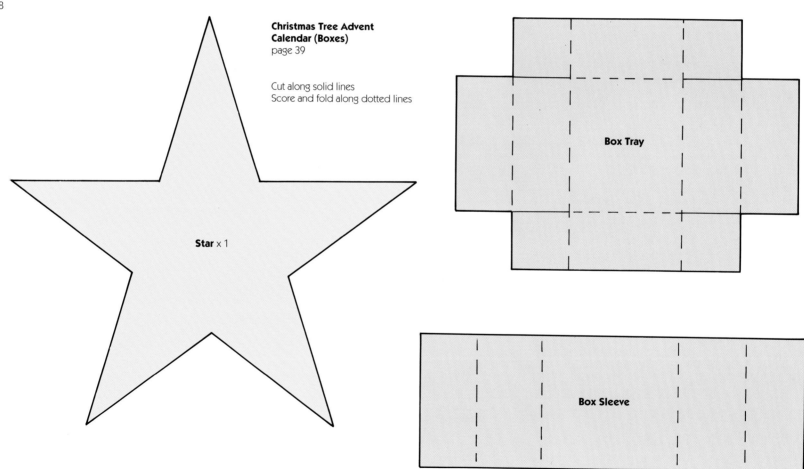

**Christmas Tree Advent
Calendar (Boxes)**
page 39

Cut along solid lines
Score and fold along dotted lines

Star x 1

Box Tray

Box Sleeve